The Real Scientist
Flash!
Light and how we see things

Peter Riley

W
FRANKLIN WATTS
LONDON•SYDNEY

Contents

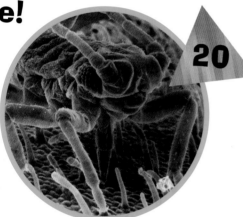
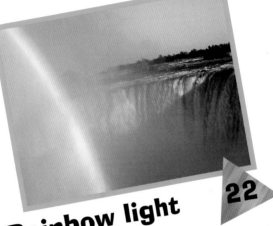

Light energy

What do we see when lightning strikes or fireworks explode in the sky? **FLASH!** There's a burst of light! Everything we see is as a result of light streaming into our eyes. No one is sure exactly what light is, because it behaves in different ways. But real scientists know that light is a form of energy. Most of the light energy that lights up our world comes from the Sun.

Light shoots across the air in an instant, moving at 300,000 metres per second straight into our eyes! Light energy is released by the Sun and other stars. It is also released when materials, like these fireworks, burn or glow.

At other times light behaves like microscopic cannon balls called photons. When photons crash into light cells, such as the ones in this solar-powered mobile phone charger, they generate electricity.

Sometimes light energy travels in waves. When sea waves crash together they get mixed up. The rainbow colours we see on a bubble surface happen when light waves collide.

How to be a real scientist

Real scientists look at our world and try to understand it by thinking about it and performing experiments. You can be a real scientist too! Just look at each topic, read the 'getting going' section and then get experimenting.

Set up a science box
Find a large box, then skip through the pages in this book and look at the things you need for getting going and for each activity. Collect them up and put them in your science box.

Use these science skills

▶ Observe
Look carefully at whatever you are investigating.

▶ Predict
Guess what will happen before you experiment.

▶ A fair test
If you are comparing how light behaves, make sure you keep everything the same in your tests except for one thing, such as the way you shine the light.

▶ Science notebook
You will need a science notebook in which to put information about your investigations.

▶ Record
Write down what happened and perhaps make a drawing in your science notebook. You could take photographs too or make a video using a camcorder or mobile phone.

▶ Make a conclusion
Compare what happened with your prediction and see if you were right. It does not matter if you were wrong because it helps you rethink your ideas.

▶ Experiments and answers
Follow the steps in the experiments carefully. Use your science skills. There may be extra experiments and a question for you to try. Check all your observations, ideas and answers on pages 28–29.

▶ What went wrong?
Science experiments are famous for going wrong – sometimes. If your experiment does not seem to work, look for this section to help you make it right.

Lights out!

Light isn't everywhere all the time. At night, the Sun leaves the sky and it becomes dark. Even in the daytime there are dark shadows. Look around you on a sunny day and you'll see your shadow. Shadows are places where some light cannot reach. They form on the side of objects that is away from the light source.

▼ These laser beams are as straight as a ruler, just like all light rays.

▼ You can often guess what something is from its shadow!

Light travels in straight lines, called rays. When light rays meet an opaque object, they cannot pass through or go round it, so a dark shadow is left on the other side. Translucent and transparent objects form weak or no shadows because they let some – or all – light through.

Getting going

Shadows shift as the Sun moves around the sky. Stand on a pavement at different times of day and get a friend to draw round your shadow in chalk. How does it change? Now try experimenting with some more shadow shapes.

Shadowy shapes

Small torch, wooden block (e.g. domino), sheets of white paper, glue, cereal box, protractor, ruler and pen, felt-tips or coloured pencils, collection of small objects (e.g. toy figure, toy car, marble), clear plastic cup or bottle.

1

Place the block at the edge of a sheet of paper. Shine the torch at it, from about 20 cm away. Move the torch closer, then further away.

2

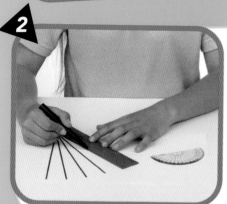

On a clean piece of paper, use the protractor and ruler to draw lines at angles of 30, 40, 50, 60, 70, 80 and 90 degrees. Stick the paper on the side of a cereal packet.

3

Line up the cereal packet with the block. Shine the torch on the block at each angle in turn, starting at 30 degrees.

4

Place an object in the centre of a piece of paper and shine the torch at it from one height but different directions. Try using other objects.

► **Observe**
Draw around the shadows in each step, using different colours. How do the shadows change each time? Can you create some cool shadow patterns on the paper? Try taking photographs of the shadows and see if your friends can guess the objects' identity.

► **Predict**
What would happen if you replaced the block with a clear plastic cup or bottle? Test your prediction.

► **Record**
Make a table and record the length of the shadow when the torch is shone at the block from 30, 40, 50, 60, 70, 80 and 90 degrees.

► **Fair test**
Keep the torch at the same distance from the object as you change the angle at which it shines.

► **Extra experiment**
Shine a large torch at a white wall or screen in a darkened room. Make shapes with your hands in front of the light. Can you make a bird or a deer shadow? Try other animals!

► **Think about it**
What would happen if you shone two torches on an object from different directions?

Clever cameras

Cameras are amazing light machines! They take in light and use it to make a picture, or photograph. When light energy enters a digital camera, it creates currents of electricity. These form a picture that is stored in the camera's memory when you click the button.

▼ **Most mobile phones have a digital camera. You can use one to record your experimenting!**

Getting going

The simplest camera is a pinhole camera. It lets in just a few rays of light through a tiny hole. The rays travel in a straight line to a screen at the back, where they form a faint but clear picture. Can you make a picture using a pinhole camera?

Pinhole pictures

1

Paint the inside of the box black and leave it to dry. Cut a large window in one end of the box, leaving a narrow frame around the edge.

2

Cut a smaller window in the other end, about 6 cm square. Put on the lid and seal it down with sticky tape so that no light can get in.

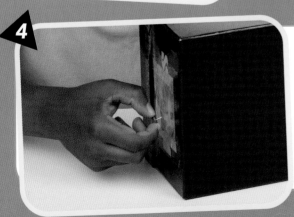

Science box

Shoe box (or other similar-sized card box) with a lid, black poster paint, paintbrush, sticky tape, scissors, greaseproof paper, aluminium foil, drawing pin, torch.

3

Tape a piece of greaseproof paper over the large window and a piece of foil over the small window.

4

Use a drawing pin to make a tiny hole in the centre of the foil. Be very careful not to tear the foil.

▶ **Observe**
Switch on the torch and point the foil end of the camera at the light. What do you see on the greaseproof paper. Move the camera closer. Describe what you see. Point the foil end of the camera at a sunny window (but not the Sun).

▶ **What's wrong?**
Can't see the sunny window? Put a shade around the screen. Make sure the box is properly sealed. Still can't see anything? Make the pinhole slightly larger.

▶ **Predict**
What would happen if you made the hole bigger? What would happen if you made two holes? Test your predictions.

▶ **Think about it**
Our eyes act like pinhole cameras to make pictures of the world. Which way up are these pictures at the back of our eyes?

Bouncing rays

Things that give out light are called light sources. They include candles, light bulbs, stars and computer screens, as well as the big one – the Sun! But most things in our world don't produce light – so how do we see them? We see them by light rays bouncing off them. Real scientists call this reflection.

You are reading this by light rays reflecting off the page into your eyes. The light source might be an electric light, or it might be sunlight through a window. Light from the Sun will have bounced off many things, such as clouds, walls and trees, before reaching you.

Getting going
Some materials reflect light better than others. Try bouncing light off your watch onto the ceiling and making it dance around! Could you do the same with your bare arm? Let's find out more about reflecting.

1

Use lumps of modelling clay to stand up the two white cards. Arrange them with the torch between, so that light reflects from one card onto the other.

2

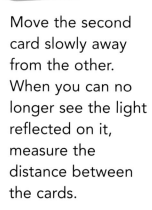

Move the second card slowly away from the other. When you can no longer see the light reflected on it, measure the distance between the cards.

These are the lists of contents for the titles in The Real Scientist: